The Women at the Well

The Women at the Well

*

Poems & A Revelation

Grace Bauer

Portals Press

Cover photo by J. Travis of sculpture by Ivan Mestrovic;
Sri Yantra on pp.15, 47, and 79; Author's first Communion, p.93.

Grateful acknowledgement to the following journals in which some
of these poems (sometimes in slightly different versions) first
appeared: *Frontiers: A Journal of Women's Studies*: "The Women
At The Well," "Lot's Daughters Bent On Revenge," and "Noah's
Wife Addresses The Department Of The Interior." *Iris*: "Mary: A
Confession And Complaint." *The MacGuffin:* "Miraculous
Women: A Triptych" and "The Prodigal Daughter's Girl."
North Carolina Humanities: "The Woman Taken In Adultery Takes
Another Chance," "Salome: The Choreography Of Guilt," and
"Mary Magdalene's Chapter And Verse." *North Dakota Quarterly:*
"Susanna: On Bathing In Light." *Poetry:* "Eve Recollecting The
Garden." *13TH Moon:* "Ruth: On Wandering. On Wonder."
"Veronica: On Troublesome Veils" appeared in *The Maple Leaf
Rag 15th Anniversary Anthology*, New Orleans, LA, 1994, Portals
Press.

Published by Portals Press
4411 Fontainebleau Drive
New Orleans, Louisiana USA 70125

ISBN 0-916620-33-6
Library of Congress Catalogue Card Number
97-66182

These poems were influenced and informed by a variety of sources beyond The Bible itself and the people who originally told me the stories it held. Those sources include *The Book Of J* by Harold Bloom, *A Dictionary of Symbols* by J.E. Cirlot, *The Complete Gospels* by Robert J. Miller (editor), *Stealing The Language* by Alicia Ostriker, *The Gnostic Gospels* by Elaine Pagels, *All The Women Of The Bible* by Herbert Lockyer, and *Congregations: Contemporary Writers Read The Jewish Bible* by David Rosenberg (editor).

I wish to thank the Virginia Tech Women's Research Institute and The Virginia Commission for the Arts, who generously supported the writing of this book. Also the Virginia Center For the Creative Arts, where many of these poems were written.

I dedicate this book to my family and to the nuns of Our Lady of Hungary School, to my poetry workshop and to Ellen, Ruth, Minrose, and Joan, who listened in the early stages. To Rick Waters and Ann Shaffran, who provided technical assistance. To Eddie Silva, Nevin Mercede, and Jane Varley — friends who provided inspiration and encouragement. To John P. Travis, who believed enough in this book to publish it, and to Brent Spencer for eagle-eye copy editing, among other things. To Keith Derhammer, who believed poetry mattered. To Ella and Roy, who took me to the hat store and the beach. And to Jacob, who is wrestling his own angels.

— G.Bauer
December 1996

TABLE OF CONTENTS

II

III

Both read the Bible day and night
But thou readst black where I read white
William Blake

Jesus met the woman at the well
And he told her everything she'd ever done
Traditional

Speaking in Tongues: An Incantation

In the beginning was water.
And the word rose out of the face
of the deep and *world* was the word

we created to name ourselves
out of the darkness.
And above us we saw an expanse

of sky, a firmament blue
as ocean, holding a circle of fire,
a crescent of ice, and they mirrored

their light in the water.
And in time dry land appeared,
so we roamed, and we discovered

thirst and distance, and names
for every *thing* that filled
the void we knew as hunger.

And we wandered the distance
from river to stream, always
leaving and returning to water.

And the land greened fertile
with grasses and trees as we learned
to plant seeds and pick blossoms.

And the land contained rock
and stones we broke open
to learn what they held

at their centers. Searching
for roots, we made a circle
of stones and dug into the earth

to find water.
And in the earth we dug
we discovered clay, and we learned

to form clay into vessels.
And the vessels, we knew,
like the stones, like ourselves,

held emptiness deep in their centers.
And we filled all the vessels
with water and oils we made

from seeds and blossoms. And we
annointed our flesh with the fragrance
of herbs and glazed our skin

smooth as fine vessels. But we felt
what we were was more
than mere flesh, something

in us ran deeper than water.
So we searched for a word
to name this thing that we felt

like an unbroken stone
at our centers.
And we saw with our eyes

and reached with our hands
toward each other
to fill up the darkness.

And we knew ourselves fertile
as the green of the earth:
tangled roots, tangled vines,

seeds and blossoms.
And we gazed at tall trees
and imagined a tower

we might raise with our hands
towards the heavens. And we
built it with stone because

we thought it would last
and could stand up to time
and to water.

And each stone held
a word, and each word
held a story, and each

story a secret, a center.
But our tower collapsed
and our children were scattered,

bearing stories like stones
in their pockets.
And now sometimes they pause

by the side of a stream
to skip stones across the mirror
of water, and they watch as

the ripples they make form
a circle that captures the light
at its center.

Look into that center:
the darkness, the light, the face
you see in the mirror.

Come close. You may well see
us lurking, familiar, like dreams
you still see upon waking.

We are the women who wait
by the wells with clay pitchers
posed on our shoulders.

We are here to draw water.
We are here to throw stones.
We are here to break

silence with story.

I

Lilith Revises Her Absence

The story begins here.
Before Eve was, I was.
Before the fractured
rib, before anyone dreamed
of apples. I was beside
Adam. Adamah. I was part
of the story. Part of the whole.

Earth-born. Whispered into
life, formed of spirit
and dust: god-mother-
sister-daughter-bride.
Other to Adam, the first man
to declare himself born
to be on top. I declared

myself the right to change
from ridden to rider
when so moved, refused to
take less than instinct and passion
would allow. Refused to take
orders that limited the body's
possibilities in love. That limited me.

I sensed what his limits were
leading to and I knew
of what I had been made,
and that to be what one is
is the only sense worth knowing.
So I fled to the sea they call
red because I saw it so.

Adamant. I refused three angels
who summoned me to submission.

Let it not be done unto me,
I swore, unless I can
also do it. Let Adam lie
with his anonymous animals
and eat his un-named fruit alone.

He was not alone long before
Eve was *erected*, you might say,
out of his bone. He awoke
to find a dream girl reclining,
docile, in my place. *This*, he thought,
is truly Paradise. But discontent
grew like kudzu in fertile ground.

The serpent, that nightmare,
grew vivid as blood in their hearts,
which grew bored by perfection.
And their minds, those untamed weeds,
imagined and desired more. Just as I had.
Just as you, admit it, always do.
This is our shame. And our glory.

This is the way of our world.
I say *our* because I am of you
and with you, no matter who tries
to write me out of the story.
Deny me if you will, I am never gone.
Revise me into your worst fears, but I am
still part of your vision. Part of you.

Call me slut or succubus,
harlot or hag, vampire or vixen,
terrible mother, merciless beauty,
the face that launched ships or turned
men into stone — or swine — whatever
men turn themselves into these days —
because who am I really, except

what they, you, we all long for and are
frightened of being? At night we lay
aside our dazzling masks, our proper
garments and sink our teeth into
the skin of raw, sweet symbol:
those stories we compose in sleep
to hide our *selves* from ourselves.

Those dark tales tellers refuse
to remember, those webs weavers
unravel in search of pattern,
order, sense — refusing to accept
their own renegade dreams for the outlaws
they are. Being the original
outlaw, I know this old story well.

And I know what courage it takes
to tell it right. Each of us comes
upon a darkness we close our eyes to.
Each of us faces a cave we fear
to explore, a shadow we run from.
But it catches us every time
with our pants down, our skirts lifted

howling like wolves in the moonlight,
screeching like owls in the woods.
Spirits out of our minds to be
in and out of our bodies. Infants laugh
in their innocent beds to hear this
mysterious music. *My* song. Ours.
The one we are all born dying to know.

Eve Recollecting the Garden

Was it your nakedness
or the knack you had

for naming I learned
to love? *Crow*, you whispered

and wings flapped black
as satin in the sky

Bee, and sweetness thickened
on my tongue. *Lion*

and something roared beneath
the ribs you claimed

you sacrificed. Our first quarrel
arose about the beast

I thought deserved a nobler tag
than *Dog*. And *Orchid* —

a sound more delicate. Admit it!
Dolphin, Starling, Antelope

were syllables you stole
from me, and you

were the one who swore
we'd have to taste those blood

red globes of fruit
before we'd find the right word

for that god-forsaken tree.

Noah's Wife Addresses
the Department of the Interior

Birds, though they sing
sweetly, can be hell
when cramped in cages.

Cats of all kinds
do not take well to boats.

All primates stink,
albeit they are clever.
Giraffes are a pain
in the neck to feed.
Try it once, you'll see.

Chickens are dumb
and geese are mean.
Swans are not always graceful.

Bears are loners. Wolves
stick with their kind,
though elephants warm up
to strangers rather fast.

The snakes weren't half
as bad as I'd imagined.
Rats — though they, too, have
their place — most decidedly were.

The insects I got used to,
though at first I forgot
and swatted a few. Lizards
are more temperamental
than turtles. Pigs make better
housemates than gazelles.

Now that we just have
a dog and a couple of goldfish,
the place seems kind of empty.
There's too little to pet.

Of the whole menagerie,
I'd say I miss the zebras most.
One dove still comes back
every Spring, though
considering the state
of affairs these days,
he is often a bit depressed.

When I think of what we
went through trying to keep
that whole damned zoo afloat —
the times I sat up all night
with a homesick horse, the time
all the deer and elk came
down with the croup . . .

Of course, when the rainbow
arced new hope on the horizon,
I thought it had all been worthwhile.

But I have watched the world
being malled, the waters
fouled, the air clouded
with *progress*, and gentlemen,

if I wasn't a God-fearing woman,
I swear, some days
I'd start praying for rain.

Lot's Daughters Bent On Revenge

He would have given us up
for strangers — his own flesh
and blood — sacrificed

our prized innocence to insure
their safety in his home.
He said it was a matter of honor.

What manner of god rewards
such lack of feeling?
Not once did we see him

hesitate or weep for the lost;
yet she who glanced back
was punished, remains

a monument to pity, captive
of a gesture of the heart.
Knowing his love

of wine, tonight we serve
him into a stupor, then put
him into service — pleasure

divorced from lust. We know this man
who's love we've never known.
And fuck his honor.

With our sons, his sons, our brothers
we return like deer
to lick our mother's salt.

Sarah: On Senses of Humor

Forgive him? Ha! I could
never forgive him. Nor could I
understand a god who demands
such tests of loyalty.

Isaac claimed the deed
was all in the past, that no
harm had *really* been
done him, but he was scarred
by the memory of that knife
at his throat. He never got over
his fear of fire — or Abraham —

who tried to make light
of his intentions that day,
pretending it had all
been a misunderstanding,
a practical joke designed
to delight a boy with terror —
like a good ghost story or
a playmate yelling *boo*!

Some joke! I don't get it.
What kind of father plays
games with his child's life?
What kind of god would want him to?

I think better evidence of faith
could be found in the simple
acts of kindness love inspires us
to perform, the giving-up that doesn't
have to feel like sacrifice.

If I commit the sin
of arrogance, it seems to me
a lesser one than murder.
Less than the hardness
of heart my husband displayed —
always so cock-sure of his
virtue. Ha! And for that
he is praised! I sometimes
think the *real* test was to see
how far a man would go
to prove himself a prophet.
If that is what it means
to be blessed, well, I'll be damned.

Call me the mother
of nations? Ha! I had only
one son and I almost lost him.
And I have laughed in the face
of my husband *and* heaven, and I will
continue laughing at the bad joke
some call justice in this world.

Rebekah Reconsiders

From Eve all mothers
learned *boys will be boys*.
One may hunt, the other plough;
one may be rough, the other gentle.
But both will be
in competition because
she calls both *son*.

And though she may love
both more than herself, she may
love one more generously, causing
pain no child should ever feel.

I am guilty of a preference
of the heart my mind could
not control, a treachery
I never should have plotted.

I suppose it was partly
that Jacob seemed so timid,
while you, Esau, were tougher
with your ruddy good looks
and roguish charm.

I misjudged, I admit.
You proved that later
with mercy, with the tolerance
you showed your brother
when he finally returned.

Though robbed of both
birthright and blessing,
you survived — a man
of dignity — living

quietly with the wounds
I helped create.

Can one expect forgiveness
at this late date?
If so, Esau, I beg it.

Look around at the men
you share this less
than glorious world with.
See how many wear a look
of long-felt sorrow
in their eyes.

Perhaps, like you,
some of them had mothers —
mortal women who did not
always treat all children well,
who made mistakes their graves
found them regretting.

You came into this life
with your brother clinging
to your heel, but grew
to walk behind him,
in the shadow of his fame.

Live well in your obscurity.
Live well and love your children.

Bestow your blessings
equally and pardon my sins
against you in their names.

Rachel and Leah Tapdance
Around Tension: A Duet

Once I had a sister.
Then I met a man.
He worked and slaved
for seven years
to pay my brother
for my hand.

But, Rachel, I was oldest.
I had to marry first.

He took you thinking
you were me and that's
what hurts the worst.

But then he kept on taking.

Yes, I know.
Don't rub it in.
Of course, he loved
me better, but . . .

I grew fertile
you stayed thin.

You grew, all right.
Like a balloon.
Again, and then again.

Seven times, to be exact.

And each time brought me pain.
So I told Jacob he could take
my maid, whose brood, by law, was mine.

She bore those brats upon my knees.

Rachel, you're so unkind.

When were you ever kind to me?
You tricked me, you deceived . . .

I thought that you got over this
when you finally conceived?

By that time, I was old and tired
and worn out from the game
I feel like you forced me to play.
You made me feel so ashamed.
You were my sister, but I hated
you and all your healthy boys.

The seventh was a daughter...

And was that any cause for joy?
We spent our lives competing
to see who could bear the most.
Our children were like trophies.
Leah, something else was lost.

Like self respect, for instance.
Or lives to call our own.

Or what we had as sisters before
we left our brother's home.
Was it worth it?

Rachel, I don't know.
We did what we had to do.

And Joseph's brothers hated him
as much as I hated you.

I spent my life trying
to win Jacob's love
and kept begetting hate.
You spent yours longing
for children and cursing
your barren state.

The great irony, of course,
is that I finally had my sons,
but by then I was so exhausted
and what was done between us
was done.

Once I said to Jacob,
"Give me sons or I shall die."
But it was giving birth
that killed me. Ben's first
breath was my last sigh.

But Joseph went on
to do great things.
You can be proud of him.

I really have no use for pride.
It's the saddest of all sins.

Rachel, can we stop this now.
We are both, at last, at rest.
Let's call a truce and lie in peace,
consider ourselves blest.

Funny, how we rest now
as we did when we were younger —
side by side and arm in arm.

If only we'd been stronger . . .

We had our share of strength,
I think, it was alternatives we lacked.
But you're right, the past is too
far gone. I'm tired of looking back.

Once I had a sister.
Then I met a man.

I'm still your sister, Rachel.
Here, give me your hand.

Miriam: Encountering Home

The morning my mother set Moses
adrift, she commanded me to crouch
among the rushes on the riverbank
and watch as the basket she had made
to bear him bobbed precariously
along the Nile's dark waters.
It seemed too great a voyage to embark
an infant on alone, but given little
choice, poor lamb, he took his
abandonment well. I see now it was strange.
He never cried till he was rescued,
delivered to dry land and royal arms.
It was as if, even then, some part of him knew:
to journey was, would always be, our fate.

Forty years. Then forty more before
he could take his leave again, though this
time among his people — a tribe
he hardly knew. Even Aaron and I,
as we walked by his side, were little
more than strangers to him. How could he know
how desperately we had waited for deliverance —
never dreaming the child we'd sailed
out of our midst would be the one to walk us
through waters we had always dreamed of crossing.

Those years he led us through sun,
through endless sand, the memory of my mother's
tears were all I had to quench my thirsts. No man,
save my brothers, ever wandered once inside
my tents, where alone nights when the moon
waxed full, I abandoned myself to a chorus
of voices that flowed through me out of nowhere,
compelling me into song. When I sang praise

Moses hung on every word, but should I sing
of the past — or worse — a day yet to come,
his face would turn a violent gray.
He looked like a man who'd been drowned.

The one time I ventured to offer advice
(I felt my loyalty had earned my right)
he stuttered vile curses upon my head, till my flesh
turned white as virgin snow and I was banished:
Abhorrent. *Unclean! Unclean!* To lament for
seven days my brother's words. He later claimed
it was *his* prayers caused God to heal me.
Did he think I could not pray myself?
Did he think when he climbed that mountian
he was closer to God than I was in my heart?

That week turned me bitter as the waters
of Marah, but rendered me, also, wiser. In solitude
I realized some songs you are meant to keep
to yourself, to tend like flowers
in a desert of silence that will flourish
only when planted close to the source
of the well from which they spring —
the clear, dark waters within us
on which we all are set to drift — away from
and toward our mother. Our own promised land.

Bathsheba: Looking Forward. Looking Back.

It was my habit when my husband
was away waging wars to ascend
to the peace of the rooftop at dusk
and bathe my skin in rosewater and myrrh.

I assumed myself alone and loved
imagining the evening I would gaze
toward the sunset and see Uriah riding
home in a cloud of dust and glory.

How was I to know a king would stoop
to take his leisure as a spy, a voyeur
too long accustomed to possessions?
When he summoned, I obeyed. Refusal

I feared would be treason. But for a woman
submission is often judged both virtue
and transgression. Faithful subject.
Faithful wife. Either way I stood condemned.

My husband's blood stained David's hands,
but the baby struck down to atone was also mine.
No child, not even Solomon in all his splendor,
ever replaced the one who died in my arms.

Years later I watched David mourn for Absalom —
his treacherous son — but he seemed to forget
our first born's innocence before he had grown cold.
I wondered then if the heart he bore was human.

Oh, but when he sang! I admit my own heart
melted when his tongue filled my ear
with lamentations and praises, when the iron hand
he ruled with stroked his lyre strings

soft as feathers. Me, he never touched
that way again, coming to me more to restake
a claim than to find — much less to give —
comfort or pleasure. Small wonder

in old age his own flesh turned ice —
cold as the shoulder he'd given so many
who had come to him offering love.
His pride earned him his impotence.

How pathetic he was with that Shunamite
he commanded to his deathbed, too blind
to see her cringe each time he insisted
on trying. And failed. She was too young

to have heard the songs of his youth.
To be seduced by his cunning with giants
or how he'd worked his way up
from a sheep pen to a throne.

Sometimes I wish I'd known him then.
That I'd been the one to spy from a rooftop
on a boy, half naked, serenading his flock.
But what use are such wishes to a woman my age?

What does a queen know of shepherds?
Except that night after night I dream
of my children's children and see looming
in their future a stable instead of a throne.

There are three strange men in this dream
and a girl who looks a lot like me.
She bows to the words of a beckoning dove.
The wind fills with the rush of his wings.

And then I wake up. Trembling in light.

The Silence of Sheba

I surpassed him from the start
in curiosity and courage. In opulence
we were a perfect match. A stalemate,
I believe, in power and ambition.
Equals in our arrogance, I'd say.

It was wisdom, of course, he was
renowned for, so knowing
a thing or two myself, I came
to him begging to learn.
Little did I know at the time
the toll some knowledge takes.

Oh, not the gold I paid
as dues — I have plenty more
where that came from — nor
the time I spent struggling
to comprehend his views.
It's the part of myself I
gave up to make room for what
I thought he might give me,
the bone-deep intuitions
he prompted me to ignore.

He taught me codes for law
and science, formulas
I memorized by rote, secrets
of his language I can speak
now as my own. But I once had
a hold on things of the spirit
I no longer can articulate.
What was centered in my heart
no longer feels whole.

Though I now dazzle both
subjects and sovereigns alike
with the complexities I seem
to grasp, it's simple loss
I am most certain of.

Though Solomon urged me
to stay, I returned with our son
and the baggage of memory
to contemplate the nature of journeys
and knowledge, to rediscover
in silence the part of me that was
harder to leave behind than home.

Delilah's Alibi

Let's face it, for a judge
the man showed precious
little wisdom — always quick
to throw his weight around,
always chasing after whores.

Then there's the scandal
with his wife — poor girl —
conveniently forgotten.
His bad jokes, his stupid riddles.
Honey, my job was a cinch.

It wasn't just the money
made me do it — though times
were tight and I *did* need the cash —
it was the challenge of beating
the big lunk in a match of wits —
not that wit was one of his
strong points. Au contraire.

First, he lied and said *fresh withs*
would do it, and behold,
my boys got seven withs. Then he lied
and said *fresh ropes*, so my boys
got them; then he said *seven locks
of hair*, so I sat down and started braiding.

I mean, any fool would have caught
on and split, but not my Sam.
He had to tempt his fate
once more, so this time
he admitted *scissors*. Fourth time
was my charm, I guess.
He couldn't raise a hand.

I've taken this bad rap
for years — but sticks and stones
can't hurt me. He was a user.
He got used. A hunter
brought down by a game.

In the end, I guess he felt
he got his revenge, ruining that temple,
taking lots of innocents down
with him — that man never did
have much style. You'll have to

excuse me now. I've got to get down
to my new salon. The clientele
is expanding; we're all the rage.
If you'd like a change of image, just call
for an appointment. I do good work
and the first cut's always free.

Ruth: On Wandering. On Wonder.

For years I listened
to her reconstruct
her homeland in story.
As she spoke, the blue
of sky there turned
sapphire, the yellow
of wheat turned gold.
The scent of fresh baked
bread that filled the houses
of her people filled me
with a hunger. And no eating
could stop the pangs.
The laughter of friends
I knew — though never having
met them — drew me to the center
of a village in my dreams.

I didn't know then how longing
transforms landscape,
how memory can revise a place
we think beyond our reach.
So when she said she would
go back, I said at once
I would go with her.

Loyalty had little to do with it.
Love? Perhaps a bit more.
But my husband was dead and I had been
long gone from my own mother's house.
It was my chance to see the world
made wider, to become part of a story
much larger than my own.

In the book, they stress the leaving
and arriving, but it is the memory
of the journey I treasure
most of all: how spectacular
a sunrise looked above a strange
horizon, how the flavor of the common
food we devoured was enhanced
by the open air, how doggedly
a mule plods on, how in your sleep
you can still ride its rhythm,
how the lilt in a foreigner's
voice brings new meaning
to the simplest *good day.*

Things turn out as they must,
I suppose. The strange becomes
familiar. What I once called home
today seems strange.
I rarely look backwards
or try to recapture what I left
behind in words, but now that Naomi
is gone, I sometimes wander alone
by the edge of the sea and try
imagining where all that water
comes from and goes, and where
it would take me if I insisted
on following once more.

Vashti to Esther

For now you're sitting pretty
on a throne I once called mine.
I never owned it, Esther.
Nor do you. Beauty and compliance
may well keep you there
forever or you may, like me,
be banished on a whim — replaced
by some fair virgin who can
easily be replaced. And if
you stay, you'll find a throne
is a cold cage, a crown wears you
down so far the sky's light
can't quite reach you in
the satin dungeon of your rooms.

In your own way, you are clever.
Good at getting what you want
by acquiescing. You saved
your uncle's neck — not to
mention your own — and the blood
of the tribe, who will continue
to fast in your memory and honor
your name. But you'll find safety
is no substitute for freedom and
honor leaves you longing for love —
the simple touch that warms
your flesh and locates the heart
in your body — and that I doubt
you will ever feel in the arms
of your husband, your king.

I say this as a woman who has
been there. I say this as a woman
who knows. And I know you have imagined
yourself in my shoes, tried on my brash
disobedience to see how it would fit.
Perhaps you will never choose
to wear it, perhaps you will fight
all urges to refuse. But swallow
every *no* in your life, and sooner
or later, one sticks in your throat.
Remember that — and me — when the moment
comes — I swear it will. And then,
having saved your uncle, your people —
I want to see you save what you
can remember of yourself.

Judith Dreaming of Her General

It's a truly grizzly business:
beheading a man. A labor
no training can prepare you
to accomplish and no triumph
can erase from your memory
once performed. I know both

what I saved and lost,
have heard many singing
my praises, but nothing drowns
out the echo of a blade
hitting bone, the cry of terror
sliced into silence. What I did

was necessary, even inspired.
There was a town at stake, a power
beyond my own forcing my hand.
But it was — it is — *my hands*
that bear the weight of the trophy.
That symbol of defeat I cannot lose.

A dozen times a day I bathe.
I change my clothes compulsively.
Still in sleep I am spattered
in scarlet and smell vaguely
of decay. Then there's his eyes
which I see everywhere, questioning

more than they accuse. At times
they appear filled with longing,
some passion I'm afraid might
be my own. I have heard some pagan
tribes devour the hearts of the enemy
when they kill. In my case

I fear the enemy's eating mine.
I drink myself half-sick
most evenings, trying to drown
his face in wine, but it rises
to the surface of every dream
I drift away on, stares out

of every mirror, every well
I peer into, hoping to catch
a glimpse of the heroine
I know I am — the woman who tricked
a general into losing his head,
who pays a heavy price for peace
and knows herself a weapon.

Susanna: On Bathing in Light

The garden that I walk in
is now fenced against
intruders' eyes. Potential
voyeurs face glass shards,
locked gates and walls
so high the sun itself
has trouble getting in.

My gardenias have dropped
their buds in the shade,
my roses turned gangly
and pallid. The lilies
and iris adapt by distortion,
twisting their stems toward
what little day the protection
I'm imprisoned by permits.

Still my husband frets
the possible. He sees
each entrance as a threat,
every visitor as rival.
Our social life is wilting
on the vine and I am bored.

I thought I had proved
my loyalty by choosing death
before dishonor. I thought all
doubts about me were disproved.
My husband swears he trusts
I'm good, but knows the world
is evil. He doesn't know
it's knowledge of that world
I crave the most.

I doubt my virtue grows
in isolation or that ignorance
breeds anything but itself.
And love most surely needs
more room, more air, more
inspiration, more — why can't he
see it — light — if it's to bloom
or bear much fruit.

Sometimes at mid-day I nap
beneath the fig tree near
the fountain where I used
to bathe. The sound of water
falling into water helps
me sleep. I drift into a dream
of distance, a space where all
the walls are glass.
Where men and women look
each other squarely in the eye
and throw no stones.

II

Mary Recalling Bethlehem

Among oxen and asses
I labored. Brought my child
to breath through blood

and pain. I had to cut
his cord myself with one
of Joseph's carving knives.

The one he used
to hollow wooden bowls.
That night I was in no mood

for visitors, but what a flock
of them I got! Strangers.
Some in rags bearing lambs.

Others in silks with treasures
and sweet herbs. All following
a light in the night sky

I, myself, had barely noticed,
though I once knew a woman
in Nazareth who read her days

by the movement of stars.
The child was adorable
like any newborn. I posed him

for his guests on the straw —
still wet, a bit sticky from the womb,
yet resplendent in his swaddling

bands with that little shock
of coal black hair — much like Joseph's,
who acted more the father

than he was, opening his heart
to this strange son he vowed to call
his own to any man who asked.

Anne: On the Darkness in Daughters

About angels I know nothing
having seen only a stream of light
that seemed to shine from no source,
having felt only a breeze
that moved no curtain. Just that.
And then my daughter bowing
to a word I couldn't hear.

Mary had always been such
a sweet girl, polite, willing
to do as she was told. Although
she *did* tend to walk with her
head at a tilt, as if she were
keeping an ear cocked to the sky.

After her announcement she grew
secretive and headstrong,
less docile yet more resigned.
She developed a terror
of pigeons, yet once I caught her
standing like a statue in the garden
with a black snake coiled around her ankle.
She was admiring it like a jewel.

Poor Joseph! He worshipped the ground
she walked on, but I think sometimes he felt
a little used. And although she was
a decent mother in her own way, she remained
somehow removed from the child.
It was I who often rocked him
when he was fretful with fever.
I who changed him, told him stories
of his people and our past.

I had no earthly chance to see him
grow to man *or* god, so though I died
professing faith, I must confess
to doubt as well. I wanted to believe
my daughter virginal and chosen, but
like any mother who knows the ways
of this world, I sometimes shook
my head and wondered what in heaven's name
could have possibly gotten into that girl?

Elisabeth: On the Sadness of Sons

No doubt a prophet
brings less sorrow
than a savior to the woman
who bears him. Still
there was an element
of sacrifice involved,
knowing he would prepare
the way only to perish
by its side.

Joy? Well, of course, I had
my share of that, though
it was always tinged
with foreboding. Always
I heard a desert
in his cries, a river
rippling in his laughter.
Never the innocence,
the delight one expects
from a child.

I remember how he'd stare
at other children like he
was looking for a sign,
an order he'd been
waiting for since the moment
he was born. But to me

he was often disobedient.
Almost rude. His father
could never find the strength
to scold him, recalling

how he'd lost his tongue
once doubting his son
would be born.

When John left home
without a word, I was
saddened, but hardly surprised.
The mother in me mourned,
though in my heart
I always knew I'd only
had my child on borrowed time.

Stories of him drifted
back to haunt me: the locusts
and honey, his rantings
on the wages of sin,
the Messiah at hand.

Like others, I sometimes
wondered *was he crazy?*
Then I'd remember
Zachariah's conversation
with the angel and I'd long
to go and meet him at the Jordan
where I would try to hear
his words with a stranger's ears.

But what son wants
to claim his mother reborn
into his own hands? Somehow it didn't
seem quite proper, so I listened
from a distance for news.

It was my cousin Mary who came
to tell me of his passing.
How he'd been served to that

royal hussy in veils. Mary said:
now, for me, the hardest part's beginning.
But I wasn't sure exactly what she meant.

I simply bowed and closed
my eyes, thinking *my part now is over,*
and went back to weaving
the shroud I soon would lie in,
feeling barren as the days before
the Baptist fought his way
out of my womb and into
the wilderness — the father
to whom he truly belonged.

Salome: The Choreography of Guilt

Shouldn't a good child obey
her mother? Fulfill her
fondest wishes even when
the outcome is blood?

I knew nothing of John
beyond rumors of a man —
maybe mad, maybe holy
dressed in badly cured hides
and eating bugs. For some reason
my Uncle Herod was obsessed —
with both John *and* me — beyond
the point my mother saw as fitting.
She had seen that look before
in my own father's eyes, watched him
shadowing me about the house.

The Baptist didn't know
the half of it. My mother had more
than her reputation to protect.
She had me and a position
of safety she'd secured for us
the only way she could.
She was queen. And as queen
she gave me orders.

And I did only what I was told.
A simple dance that raced
the heartbeat of a king.
I did it well enough to earn
the trophy I was granted, though
really, I could never call it mine.

It was *her* desire I satisfied
with my infamous performance.
Her desire to take the head
of the man who had condemned her
and hold it, like a sick child,
in her bloody, royal arms.

The Prodigal Daughter's Girl

She can't imagine I was ever young
and longed for all-night parties,
travel, boys. She tells me
times have changed. I say *not much*
and insist on her propriety, though
I know she thinks I'm mean
and hates my caring. Perhaps I have
protected her too long, shielded her
too thoroughly from the tongues
that clucked bad omens at her birth.
How can she understand the haunting
of my father's eyes, how they clouded
with shame when I returned to his door,
back from a year's adventure.
My wild oats following me home.

I can still see him scanning the street
for nosey neighbors while I, faint
and famished, though big as a house,
clutched his unforgiving hand. My mother
fed me warm milk and bread and tended
me with kindness, but she hid her face
in her veils when she walked through
the village, until the day she ran,
bareheaded, yelling for the mid-wife,
who scowled at my pains and left
abruptly when her work was done, saying
another girl, as she gathered her coins.

She asks me very little of her father,
perhaps knowing, despite her innocence,
that I have little beyond passion
to tell of. Still, I think she seeks him out
in the eyes of every gangly boy who sings
to her sweetly or offers to help her

fetch water home from the well.
The stark pleasure of her smile
confirms my worst fears. Yet how long
can I keep her from feeling what she will —
what I once felt myself? I pray
she may be right about the times.

But in the town that has sprung up
around our village, I see too many
women wandering in rags, their few
possessions stuffed in sacks and wagons.
Some talk to themselves in low
conspiring voices; some scream endless
curses at the sky; some huddle in doorways,
silent, nursing bottles of cheap port
or their own aching arms. They look so
familiar they frighten me into blindness.
I step past them as if they were shadows
that will disappear with the sun.

My daughter once called one a pig —
the only time I ever slapped her.
She ran away then for three days
I spent regretful and sleepless.
When she came back, I wept
into her hair like a baby. I fixed her
roast veal, her favorite, and opened
a good bottle of wine. Drunk that night,
like giddy sisters, we laughed
and raised our cups to a summer moon
that rose full and circled by a faint
blue haze. Its light touched something
in both of us, igniting dreams
we share but need to keep to ourselves.
Since then, I let her stay out as late
as she wishes, trusting what is free
to leave will most often welcome returning.

The Woman Taken in Adultery
Takes Another Chance

I keep these stones arranged
around my bed — commemorative
angels guarding passion
night and day. They remind
me of what love can come
down to in the hands
of cold, self-righteous men
who would punish a woman
they desire themselves for giving
in to her own desires.

Hypocrites! They allowed
their friend — my lover —
to slink out the back door,
wanting only me to use
as evidence — a half-naked
truth they could twist into
condemnation of the strange
young man whose words they abhorred
much more than our common sin.

Like most girls my age, I had not
learned to read, but I can
still see the letters he scrawled
in the dirt — a cryptic design
I have tried for years to translate
into meaning in my dreams.

Whatever he spelled
sent my accusers shuffling,
hang-dog, home. Not one of them
rising to meet his challenge
to be the first to cast

the death-pitch each had planned,
though I could almost feel
their fingers trembling, their palms
aching to throw.

So I gathered these souvenirs
of my salvation and arranged
them into this altar
on which we now rest. I take comfort
in lying down each night among
the crude weapons they laid down.
Go ahead. Touch one. They feel
like small warm bodies. Smooth
as weathered bone, my love,
and harder than you to deny.

Miraculous Women: A Triptych

One: Jairus' Daughter Raised From The Dead

I was twelve. A mere girl.
And though already betrothed
to a stranger, I was more
enthralled with dolls
than the mystery my body was.
As my parents tell the story,
I collapsed one day without warning.
Fell into a swoon deep as a well.
From a distance, I could hear
my mother weeping, feel my father
press his ear against my heart.
Sleep surrounded me — a thicket,
a forest I could neither enter
nor leave, an irresistible garden
of roses whose dark thorns
pricked my fingers raw.

Out of nowhere came a man
with a voice like a prince.
He whispered *Maid arise!*
And rise I did! I wanted him
to kiss me, but he pressed only
wine-soaked bread to my lips.
Then he disappeared.
I never even caught his name.

Three days later I discovered blood.
I was appalled. My mother told me
of the curse. I blamed that prince.
And since then have a lot of trouble
sleeping, fearing dreams of him
will wake me to new wounds.

Two: The Bride At Cana

Perhaps the heat made me
so thirsty, or simply
the excitement of the day.
I looked across the table
toward the man my father had
chosen for me and gulped wine
till my head began to spin.

As I recollect the moon
that night rose full and bathed
the room in red. Our guests
grew raucous, breaking into song.
Men slapped my husband
on the back and leered in
my direction. My sister
stroked my hair beneath my veils.

I wasn't dumb. I'd watched both
sheep and dogs mate, and once
pulled a still-born calf from
its mother's womb. But to picture
myself, naked, lying
in a naked stranger's arms —
I blushed just to imagine it
and drained another glass.

With such scenes on my mind
I never saw the Nazarene arrive,
trailed by uninvited guests.
Twelve, my mother claims.
She didn't mind. There were fruits
and breads, and meat enough to last
all night, but when our flasks
ran dry, she was dismayed.
My cousin from Jerusalem —

a nasty drunk — demanded more.
For once I felt like I was
on his side. The Nazarene
stared calmly at the ceiling
for a moment, then sighed, reached
for a water jug and poured.
The crowd inhaled in unison
when water flowed the color of blood.
He handed me a glass. It tasted sweet.

Next morning I awoke to watch
my husband sleeping at my side.
He looked about as haggard as I felt.
Still I loved the way his lips
half-parted, the way his lashes
fringed his eyes. I touched myself
to see if I felt changed.

Some people claim our wedding
was one of those nights
they will never forget. I can't
forget a night I don't recall.
My husband loves me — timidly.
He's never touched a drop again.
And me? I've learned to drink
what fills my cup.

Three: Woman Cured Of An Issue Of Blood

Twelve years I bled. Continually.
Uncured by all the midwives' herbs.
Considered one *sick of her flowers*
although the bread I kneaded continued
to rise and no milk ever spoiled in my presence.
I grew hysterical. Reduced to skin and bones.

Desperation made me bold enough
to touch a man who might be God.
I thought with so many surrounding him
he would hardly feel my laying on
of hands, but the coarse-spun
cotton of his robes seared my fingers
like a flame. I gasped in pain but knew
at once I would never bleed again.

He called me *daughter*, though we
were no kin, and said my faith
had made me whole. How could I
tell him I was still plagued
by doubts? Though blessed now,
I feel an emptiness, an absence
I'm afraid to name. Can I unmake
this wish touch made come true?

Pilate's Wife Welcoming Nightmare

I dread my husband's hands
on me these days, the rough
palms and gnarled fingers raw
from so much scrubbing —
as if he could be so easily
cleansed of guilt. He knows
not even what he does. Or why.

I refrain from saying
I told you so, but didn't I
warn him of the troubled dreams
I saw at once were omens:
First, three green birds
rising toward a black sun, then
seven red roses melting in a stream

and finally, myself in white upon
a desolate hillside, spreading
my arms as if about to fly —
when, suddenly, that silent Jew
he had scourged to please
the crowd that day was there
with me. He nodded. Waved me on.

I knew not what these visions
meant, but knew they must
mean something — some *thing*
here was simply too great to ignore.
But ignore my husband did. Laughing
my intuition off as moodiness
or indigestion. He prides himself

on being calm and cunning, just
as he prides himself on cleanliness —

not seeing that obsession lies
behind his new-found urge to wring
his hands like so much sopping cloth.
I love him still, but can no longer
bear his touch, having dreamed

his flesh these past three nights
fallen from his bones. His skull
leers much too close behind
the lips he tries to press
to mine, and my desire is quenched
by a weariness that puts out
fire far quicker than the water

he plunges his arms into night
and day. I think it's blood
he still feels on his hands.
I close my eyes, hoping to find
that stranger on the hill again.
This time, I will let the dark winds
take me. And I don't care where I land.

Martha to Mary: The Quotidian Demands of the Flesh

I remember well when Jesus
said we do not live
by bread alone, but I *don't*
think he was telling us
we need not ever cook!

If the body is to rise
it must be nourished.
If it's to be nourished
well, it must be fed.

And once it eats
there are plates that must
be washed clean. To wash them
water must be fetched from wells.

To bake the bread
there's flour, which must
be sifted. Seeds must be
planted to make wheat
for flour. And food leaves
crumbs which must be brushed
from tables, or there will be
mice who will scatter
crumbs on floors.

Don't think I never
felt the urge to hang
up my apron and join
the men who sip wine
as we serve them, debating
scripture while we're out
dressing lambs.

But if we don't, tell me
who on earth *will* do it —
the never-ending work
that must get done.

Fires burn out.
Clothes rip and must
be mended. Milk spoils and
carpets do not sweep themselves.

I work my fingers
to the bone and never
get a thank you. A little
help from you, it wouldn't hurt!

The lilies of the field
are fine, and dust to dust's
poetic, but sister, what
we've got here's just plain dirt.

Mary to Martha: The Theological Insignificance of Dust

Why fret your white gloved
fingers soiled with what
we'll *both* someday become?

Smash the dishes.
Melt the copper.
Let the fabric of our tunics
rot with sweat.

Let the garden go
to weeds, which after all,
are only flowers that persist
without our planting.

If our guests want bread
direct them to the kneading.
If they want wine, then
let them fill the jugs.

Don't burden me
with details or fault
my desire to sit at the side
of the man who opened
our own brother's grave
and bid one on his way
to dust to rise and return
to the untidy world he loved.

Mary Magdalene's Chapter and Verse

It may have been more
than mere irony that
a so-called *fallen woman*
was the first allowed
to see a risen God.

I had known seven devils
and enough men to recognize
pure spirit when it came
to me, though for a moment
even his mother was
reluctant to let her
virgin heart rejoice.

And those eleven so-called
chosen few — they wrestled doubt
till they could lay
their hands on His skin.
It took open wounds to convince them.
It took the sight of blood.

I have never let them forget
their hesitation, because
I believe our Master
left a message for us here.

I think His stay among us
made Him feel passion
has its place in Paradise.
Perhaps, like me, He realized desire
is not so very far from faith.

Some men, after all these years,
still stone my tainted past
but I heave them back
the rock of their disbelief,
and ask whose load drags
heavier into heaven.

They have yet to find
an answer they can live with,
so they hand me the oldest lines
in the book. I laugh them off.
If you ask me, their apple's
sour grapes. I know they wish
they had been there
for that first *Hallelujah!*

To witness the radiance
that filled the tomb
as I have described it
again and again, so they will
always remember how
this fallen woman, who once cradled
His cold, human flesh
in her arms, in that moment
rose above them, with a glimmer
of light they dream of
seeing hereafter, held now
and forever in her
dark sinner's eyes.

The Other Mary Claims Her Name

Neither virgin nor harlot,
not taken by many men
nor chosen by a singular god,
never possessed nor blessed
with a wealth of possessions,
just a woman like most
making her way through
a life in which love and faith
intersect for a moment in light.

I survive almost nameless.
Little mention beyond Matthew's
reference to *Mary Magdalene*
and the other Mary, sitting
over against the sepulchre,
a brief mention of my sons.
Not even my full fifteen
minutes of fame. If I struggled
in raising my family,
how I felt about their following
the Lord, all this has been
lost to *His* story, the one
some call the greatest ever told.
Perhaps it is. And then again, perhaps
it is only the one told most often.

The ones who carry the body
into the world within
their bodies, the ones
who nourish and nurture the body
from their bodies, the ones
whose bodies become icons
for *the body,* who prepare
the bodies of the dead and mourn

them most, even those who find the dead
risen into prophecy — all these Marys
merge, like me, into the anonymous.

But we find comfort in oblivion.
And company. A lovely crowd recalling
our stories over cheese and bread
we have baked ourselves.
Wine that remains wine
and leaves us drunk with knowledge
of the parts we have played.
Parts which have been nearly forgotten
by those who never rose before
sunrise to greet the strange angels
who proclaimed the future had come
to pass in the dark while most men slept.

Mary: A Confession and Complaint

Legend shows me acquiescent.
Don't believe a word. I would have ignored
that angel if I could have, but he made me
an offer I couldn't refuse.
Even now I blame my failing vision
on those few moments of terrifying light.

I was not an ambitious girl.
I loved Joseph and looked forward
to our marriage and children, who would grow
and in their time, have children.
Our days, I assumed, would be simple.
Joseph in his shop, me in my kitchen.
At night we'd share the better moments.
I would shine beneath his
hands like polished wood.

It wasn't fair to ask me to bear all that
pain without ever knowing pleasure.
And if I could have only one child,
I would have much preferred a girl.
My son, though I know he loved us,
was never affectionate. He moved
as if his body were not his own.
He had a cold, distant look in his eyes.

And Joseph, though he was always kind
and never doubted me, could not get close
to the boy. He grew more silent
with the years, more sullen.
And I could never bring myself to say
forget about the angel! Or to confess
the desire he might have found in me
if he had dared to look
beyond the piety, beneath the veils.

Veronica: On Troublesome Veils

I had never seen the man
before that moment, though
I'd heard about the preacher
who was causing such a stir
around town. Nor was I one
to attend an execution.
I considered it distasteful
to gawk like a vulture at death.

That morning I was minding
my own business. I had shopping,
several errands to run.
But there was such a commotion
in the city, such passion
in the crowds, it caught me up.

Next thing I knew, a prisoner
fell before me — a sad-looking soul
with dark, unearthly eyes
that seemed to see right
through me into depths
I hardly even knew I had.

Beneath the sweat and blood
and thorns, I could tell
he'd once been handsome —
not that *that* should matter,
but the fact stays with me now
despite the horror of the image
he left with me. Here it is —
a veil like any other. At least
it *was* until it touched his face.

Stains I would have expected —
although white vinegar and salt
can take out blood — but look
how they're composed upon
the fabric, distinct
as Caesar's profile on a coin.

I've thought of soaking it
to take away the odor, but
I'm afraid I'd fade the picture
as well — although, God knows,
that *might* be a blessing . . .

If I hang it on a wall, I swear
his gaze seems to trail me.
If I fold it in a closet, I swear
I hear him weeping in the dark.
I can't wear it anymore
because the smell of blood
overpowers me, yet

I feel, somehow, responsible
for this remnant, this flimsy
miracle that weighs me down
like a cross I'll be dragging
behind me long after I'm gone.

The Women at the Well

We enter on cue, bearing
prophecy, earthen vessels
waiting to be filled, directions
to the homes of fathers, brothers,
husbands who always take
you in and treat you well.

And we are taken in by your telling:
tales of how one learns to walk
in a foreign land, moments past
recalled by one who never watched
them happen, plots still being
written in which we wait
for our names to appear.

We hear most when we are least
observed, so we are often silent,
serving the choicest meats
from our larders, the saltiest
olives, sweetest breads, red wines
from deep in our cellars, where we
carefully rinse the bottles clear of dust.

Always we fill your cup before
it is quite empty. We have learned
how to keep strangers talking,
our own thirsts quenched.
This is what keeps us returning
each day to the circle of women
drawing buckets from the circle
of stone at the center of town.

We soak clothing, refresh weary
livestock, wet our lips, composing
our own stories as we wait
for our reflections in the mirror
of water to speak
what we have always known.

III

Revelations:
On Hearing My Voice Among Others

I don't recall ever really *deciding* to do this. It just sort of happened. Or I just started letting it happen. It began, innocently enough, with a single poem. The subject was Mary. As in *the* Mary. The Virgin with a capital V. God's mom. A very mortal woman as I pictured her — or *heard* her, to be more precise.

The poem began, as many of my poems do, with a phrase out of nowhere: *don't believe a word.* As in *the* Word! In the beginning was the . . .! Let it be done unto me according to thy . . .! The Word made flesh! But it was the flesh that concerned me in the poem. It was the mom. The girl from the small town expecting the ordinary and getting anything but. The woman whose life was — well, *disrupted*, I should think, by a miracle — the distinction of being chosen. It was her story seen through the eyes of a cynic who can't give up believing in miracles despite her doubts, the believer who knows that in her own day and age, a girl with a miraculous story like Mary's *could* not be believed — by her or anyone. Probably not tolerated. Undoubtedly submitted to a cure for her delusions. *Madonna*, after all, is a word that will never quite be the same.

My intentions in writing the poem were surely not to be blasphemous, though I was fully aware that having Mary admit to missing passion might raise some eyebrows. The nuns who first brought the story to life for me at Our Lady Of Hungary School would, no doubt, flip their veils, turn in their graves. But I *had* to let Mary be human. Be a woman. Be more than a little like me. And so she was.

....

For nine years I spent the greater part of my days — Monday through

Friday, September through May — in the hallowed confinement of Our Lady of Hungary School. Although as a child, I was immersed in a hodgepodge of what we would now call "ethnic culture," I didn't know it at the time, and so, until about the fourth grade, I thought this "Lady" of "Ours" had more to do with food than with the eastern European country where many of the parishioners were born.

Our Lady of Hungary School stood next to a church of the same name, which stood on a block of churches. Ours was huge and gothic with three large altars — white, filled with statues of saints — all female on the left, which was known as the "women's altar," and all male on the right, which was, of course, known as the "men's." The middle and largest altar held the monstrance and consecrated host plus a crucifix. It was the center of attention, and yet now it is the one I remember least. What other saintly paragons stood there? I will have to think — or ask. I can't re-visit, since the church has undergone major renovations and the beautiful old altars have been replaced in the name of progress.

Directly across the street from Our Lady of Hungary, or the "Hunky Church," as it was usually called, was the Assumption of the Virgin Mary Ukrainian Orthodox church with its silver onion spire and a cross with an extra crossbar slanted though its heart; and down the block was Saint John the Baptist — another Ukrainian church — the one my great grandmother went to the once a year she came into town to do her Easter duty.

It was at that school on that seemingly blessed block that I first heard the stories I'm now compelled to try to make into poems. The nuns, my primary sources, would tell them as if they had been there, embellishing a scene when they felt it necessary in order to make a point. The point they usually wanted to make was for us to behave and do as we were told. Each tale boiled down to a moral, an admonishment to commit no sins — which it seemed to me most things were.

Though I now appreciate the nuns' talent for story more than I ever thought I would, I also realize that many of their morals required them to delete a lot from the plot as it comes down to us in *The Good Book* — not that I'd ever read it then. *The Bible* to me was a leather volume kept in a cedar chest with Baptismal gowns, wed-

ding veils and souvenirs my uncles had brought back from Korea —
satin baseball jackets and porcelain dolls, which were ours, and yet
kept from us — things to be saved. The Bible was where my grandmother kept birth certificates, marriage licenses and deeds to her burial
plot. And so, to me, the stories were part of an oral tradition carried
on faithfully by the nuns — and, of course, the priests, who read a
brief passage at every Mass. The nuns though, in my experience, told
the stories better. Freed from the written text, they ad-libbed with
both passion and aplomb. The rhythm may have been King James, but
the accent I knew the stories in was often German or Hungarian, and
each voice, each teller, gave the stories a decidedly different timbre
and flare. I never thought then those voices would come back to
haunt me. Those nuns now serve as muses despite me. Despite themselves.

....

My *O.E.D.* informs me the word *persona* comes from the Latin word
denoting *mask*. But what kind of mask is it that I try on in these
poems? Who precisely is disguising whom? And for what purpose?
I work out the answer poem by poem. The voices keep echoing each
other. There's a recurrence of themes like anger, water, light, sin and
stones. A lot of puns that perhaps only I will know are there. A few
jokes that no one but me may find amusing. I've taken to talking out
loud to myself more than usual as I write them. After I've spent a few
hours working on them, I tend to feel a little schizophrenic, yet I
worry that some of the voices in the poems sound too much alike. I
think this may be the kind of book that will *insure* that I never get an
NEA — if the NEA survives. Senator Helms would, no doubt, find
them offensive. It's not a crucifix in pee by a long shot, but it is surely
way beyond anything he would deem acceptable. And free speech be
damned.

....

At Our Lady of Hungary, there was one particular nun who'd been
there, I think, since the school's very founding. She'd taught my

mom. She'd taught my dad. If I had stayed in town and lived as she'd instructed me to, she would, no doubt, have taught my children. But I strayed. Sister Ruth had a line of advice she'd passed on to God-knows-how-many seventh-grade girls. It was: *the greatest thing a girl can ever grow up to be is a virgin.* I think most of us took her advice to heart until we learned what such a career entailed. Then I thought it was kind of shabby to define yourself by what you did *not* do. Especially when what you did not do was IT. The deed the nuns could only bring themselves to refer to obliquely as *acts of impurity.* We were instructed continually on how to avoid such acts. One nun suggested we take baths in our underwear to avoid arousing *impure thoughts.* Another warned us if we aroused such thoughts in boys, we were sinning double. Though their thoughts were out of our hands, the blame for them, it seemed, was on our heads. One nun went so far as to say if a girl got raped, she had *two* black marks (her metaphor for sin) on her soul: one for her own act of impurity and one for the loss of the boy's soul, which she had caused.

For years after I'd strayed from the path they had mapped out for me, I chalked up the misogyny of these instructions to the nuns themselves. They were old-fashioned women. Some of them immigrants from *The Old Country*, a place they spoke of with a nostalgia that rivaled Adam's regrets over Eden or Moses' longing for the Promised Land. Surely, I thought, the "Good Book" didn't espouse rules and judgments that seemed so obviously bad. But now that I'm reading it on my own, I wonder. Too many of the so-called Biblical heroes seem to me to have, not only feet of clay, but hearts of vipers. Paul sounds like an unrepentant misogynist. Abraham and David, self-righteous and self-serving. It seems to me their egos are often out of control. They're not the kind of guys you'd want as friends — except for maybe David who, despite his faults, might grace you with a song. My favorites from the male cast of characters are Joseph, who gets far too little credit or attention, and Luke, without whom Christmas just wouldn't be the same.

As for the women, no doubt about it, I often like the bad girls best and feel the urge to come to their defense. Nowhere in *Genesis* does it say that Eve twisted Adam's arm when it came to those apples. Bathsheba, too, I think, gets a bad rap, since David was the one with the power. Vashti had a lot more integrity than Esther. Magdalene more *chutzpa* than all the apostles combined. And so I write them into poetry. Slip their masks on and lose myself in monologues that keep me circling my office, my living room, my studio — depending on where I am — reading and re-reading scriptural passages. Consulting books — from the controversial *Book Of J* to Christian instructional volumes on how to be more like _____(fill in the blank) or how and why *not* to be like_____ (ditto).

These Biblical women are held up as models of good and evil. And yet consistency does not seem to be one of the strong points of the narratives. The God of this book is finicky to say the least. While submission may get you glory one time (Esther, say. Or Mary), another time all it gets you is disgrace and a son who grows up smart though not always kind. (i.e.Bathsheba) Damned if you do and damned if you don't seems to be the recurring message. What's a girl to do?

....

My life as a writer really started back there at Our Lady of Hungary school. I have evidence of that — a couple of marble-fronted notebooks with essays like "My Favorite Martyr" (Saint Agnes, I claimed, though now I don't remember her story). The notebook also contains some rhymed and metered "odes" to things like Autumn and Jack Frost. I don't remember writing these things. But I do remember a bit about the girl who went to Mass every day before school in her blue serge uniform and white blouse that was supposed to be crisp and unwrinkled, but in my case, never was. I remember how enthralled she/I was with the ritual, the music, the smell of frankincense, the glow of candles in their little red glass cups. Once, I remember my best friend, Karla, and I got in trouble because we went into church one afternoon and lit every single vigil light we found. Somehow the nuns saw this as stealing or irreverence for the dead, for whom the candles were traditionally offered, but it was, I know, an attempt to experience beauty — a truly spontaneous spiritual act.

Studying poetry at Our Lady consisted of memorizing verses for alternate Friday afternoons; on the intervening Fridays we had "art," which consisted of each student in the class tracing and drawing the identical picture — usually determined by the seasons or an upcoming holiday. This "art" would then be used to frame the blackboards and a student was considered "good" at "art" if she or he could make his or her picture indistinguishable from anyone else's. I was not considered very good at art.

On poetry days, we read and recited in unison — verses by poets like Henry Wadsworth Longfellow, Alfred Lord Tennyson, and James Whitcomb Riley. I loved doing this, hearing our sing-song voices chant the words like litanies, but for a long time I thought that, except for Emily Dickinson, all poets were dead white guys with three names.

When a woman like Emily did write a poem, it was about her fear of snakes (inherited from Eve, I figured). Or she announced "I'm nobody. Who are you?"

....

The Bible contains a lot of "nobodies." *All The Women Of The Bible,* an encyclopedic volume I have consulted on occasion, despite the fact that the gloss on the women and their stories offered by the author, Dr. Herbert Lockyer, (who is decidedly anti-Catholic) are sexist beyond belief, lists dozens of "wives of_____," "daughters of_____," "sisters of_____," "concubines of_____," and "women of_____," (fill in the blanks). I can't help wondering about them — all these women remembered only for their attachments. The Bible is a book filled with "stern bearded patriarchs and women with pitchers on their shoulders," says Phillip Lopate in his essay in *Congregations*. It's those often nameless women that get to me. And those pitchers. Those vessels, those objects to be filled.

It is quite natural, I suppose, that a lot of the women's stories involve those pitchers. A lot of Biblical stories — meetings, marriages, miracles — take place at wells. Those wells are, both literally and metaphorically, women's places. The women are always *fetching*. Always drawing, and perhaps drawn to, water. Water, with all its implications — Jungian, primordial.

It's July, 1991. I've been for five days writing now at the Virginia Center For The Creative Arts — "a working retreat for writers and artists" that's like a little bit of heaven on earth. Today, it is hotter than hell, but I still feel blessed. Outside my window a herd of holsteins graze, unaffected by the cacophony of typewriters that click at different rhythms; the opera that blasts out one window where a painter is intent on her work; the Chilean folksongs that drift through the closed door of a poet recalling his travels there from a studio next to my own. We've talked about our work and he's taken to leaving messages in my mailbox on occasion. Yesterday he wrote: "Have you thought of doing Hannah? The only woman in the Bible whose name spells the same forward and back?"

I hadn't thought of that angle, but I do now. The idea of a palindromic heroine sounds intriguing, and I've always liked the name. I make a note to thank him for his inspiration and to look Hannah up.

As I write that, the language suddenly strikes me as funny: these women I'm "doing," these women I say I'm "looking up" as if I'm searching a phone book in a strange city for the name of a friend I haven't heard from in years. In a way, it *does* sometimes feel like that's what I'm up to. Some of these characters were so much a part of my childhood imaginative world, they *do*, in some sense, feel like friends — even though some of them were presented to me as cautionary tales. Women I wouldn't want to be. But I think I *always* saw it differently. More than morals, I saw characters — people — women and girls whose lives were somehow related to my own. When I thought of someone like, say, Salome, I saw that while she might not be someone to "look up" *to*, she certainly wasn't boring, and I knew she certainly had a story beyond that one night on the dance floor. Somehow in my head I think I connected her with the dance contests they used to have on *American Bandstand* — a show I was addicted to. I'd run home from school to catch those teenagers, many in Catholic school uniforms similar to my own, twisting and strolling to the latest hits. *Couple Number One. Let's hear the applause. Couple Number Two.....*until the winners were chosen. I don't remember what prizes those lucky couples won. 45's maybe, or trips to Atlantic

City. Salome's trophy is, of course, unforgettable.

The VCCA is just outside of Lynchburg, VA, home of Jerry Falwell and the Moral Majority. I wonder what he would think if he knew that just down the road some poet was reworking stories he's used in his own sermons? I worry that some of the poems may sometimes sound a bit like sermons of my own. Other times I feel that might not be so bad. Yesterday I "did" a draft of Miriam. Moses' sister. A character who, I discovered through my research, is considered by some the first woman poet in the Bible because of the Song she and Moses sing after the incident with the Egyptians and The Red Sea — one of my favorite scenes from — I think it was *The Ten Commandments* — where Yul Brynner played Pharaoh and the "water" looked like satin curtains billowing in fake wind. Miriam — a name close to Mary. Poet — that was my hook. Hannah, on the other hand, seems to be one of those who got away. I can`t find her voice.

Today I'm working on Bathsheba. A character I like more than I'm supposed to. I see her as a woman stuck between a rock and a hard place. After all, how does one say no to a king? How *could* one say no to one of the greatest poets of all time? But like a lot of poets, David developed an ego, and I wonder if it's *my* ego that somehow keeps me from getting Bathsheba right. I try to talk my way through a third stanza, keeping my voice down, so the poet next door won't be distracted from his imaginitive sojourn into Chile, where he is worrying about bottles and stones. The painter with the opera wouldn't hear me if I screamed. The cows wouldn't care.

....

It's been seven years since I wrote the Mary poem. For a long time, it sat in a folder with a lot of other poems that didn't quite fit into the manuscript I was working on, so it sat in a drawer awaiting — what?

About four years after Mary, Eve whispered, as it were, in my ear: *was it your nakedness / or the knack you had for naming / I learned to love?* Now I had two poems that didn't fit anywhere, except together. The lightbulb had not yet turned on, but I was getting near the switch. Perhaps, I said to myself, I could write a series of poems that would help these two oddballs fit somewhere.

At the time, I thought "series" meant a half-dozen poems or so, enough to make a tidy little section of a book. Twenty-eight poems later, I am still writing, still thinking of Biblical women who deserve a voice of their own. Not that "deserving" has a whole lot to do with it. Often, I will begin reading, taking notes, trying lines, *certain* that I want to make a poem about a particular character — only to find I just can't get her to speak, or find a way to speak for her — I'm still not sure how the process works. Sometimes another character will scream so loud, she drowns out my original intention. Lot's daughters, for instance, insisted — I'm not trying to be cute here — they really seemed to *insist* that I write about them, instead of their statuesque mother. Some, like Vashti, who were apparently outside the good sisters' Biblical repertoire, seem to jump out of the Concordance, saying, *me, hey, do me.* I accommodate when I can.

It has been a learning experience to write poems that grow, not only out of my own life, but also out of a tradition (literary, religious, cultural) that goes back centuries. I know there is much that is rich in this tradition, but I think I am beginning to see that there is much in it that is making us poorer. The God of this book — or those who have interpreted and claimed to speak for this God — got us where we are today — to a world where both women and the earth — the two often being equated — exist to be dominated. Subdued. They do not call them the *patriarchs* for nothing. We have been following their rods and their staffs, and often, we have found little comfort.

And so sometimes, the women of *this* book — or the woman who interprets and claims to speak for them — tries to turn the mythological tables, tries to stand the stories on their heads so we can get a slightly different perspective on the matter. So, for instance, I let Noah's wife — who doesn't even get the courtesy of her own name in *Genesis*, even though you can bet she was the one who was cleaning up most of the shit all those months on the ark — walk into an office in Washington, D.C. and tell her story to another group of patriarchs, who swear they have our best interests at heart.

I worry sometimes about offending people with these poems — not the Falwells, who offend *me* on a regular basis, but decent people who hold these stories dear. Other times I think we all deserve to be offended. And there is much about these stories I, myself, hold dear. I don't claim my interpretation is any truer than anyone else's — I only claim it as *an* interpretation. A perspective. Mine. I use the original story as a rock from which to jump — or fly. I make the changes my muse demands. When it suits me — or her, or him — I downright lie. Or perhaps I should say I tamper with the facts — whatever "facts" means in this context.

....

Wells: Sources. Centers. Rings. Reflections. Springs. Watering holes. Something to sit beside. To dip into. Fall into. To drop one's golden ball into, if one has a golden ball. Or one's spindle. Or pennies when making a wish. Something to be dug. A spot found with a divining rod. *Dig here.* A place from which empty vessels come back filled. A place to cleanse. To quench. To weep and add one's tears to the larger whole. A place to contemplate. Or drown. As J. E. Cirlot says in *The Dictionary Of Symbols*: "The well is also a symbol of the soul, and an attribute of things feminine." Or Eliot — from Julian of Norwich — *And All shall be well And / all manner of things shall be well.*

....

It is August, 1992. I have come here to Fairy Stone State Park with the intention of finishing this book. I want to be done with these women. They've been talking my ear off for too long. Sometimes I cannot hear my own voice speak — but maybe that is the power of myths and legends. As archetypes they can add resonance; as stereotypes they can silence our voices. The Virgins and Whores, Maidens and Crones. Mothers. Daughters. Queens and Concubines. Beauties, Bad Girls, and Bitches. They breathe not only in these stories, this book, but in some semblence, in all the stories, books, songs, lives we have known or are likely to know. We know them well.

I came to this park by default. I wanted to go to one called Hungry Mother — thinking the name auspicious for the occasion of finishing a project such as this, but the cabins were all booked-up there, so I found one here. Even more auspicious, as it turns out. According to the brochure they hand each visitor at the entrance gate, the park is named for the stones indigenous to the area, which are shaped, get this, like little crosses. The brochure says:

Many hundreds of years before Chief Powhatan's reign, fairies were dancing around *a spring of water,* (emphasis mine) playing with naiads and wood nymphs, when an elfin messenger arrived from a city far away. He brought news of the death of Christ. When these creatures of the forest heard the story of the crucifixion, they wept. As their tears fell upon the earth, they crystallized to form beautiful crosses. When the fairies disappeared from the enchanted place, the ground about the spring and the adjacent valley was strewn with these momentos of the event. For many years, people held these little crosses in superstitious awe, firm in the belief that they protected the wearer against witchcraft, sickness, accidents and disasters.

I wonder *why* the fairies disappeared. Where they went. Or why. What happened to the spring? There is a lake here, but it is is man-made and covers a town that once was thriving. Be that as it may, the legend of the fairies seems to enchant this place for me, although it seems mosquitos have replaced them for the most part. I like the fact that I'm finishing, or trying to finish, my stories in a place that has a story of its own. I ignore the geological explanation about staurolite crystals naturally forming these miniature Christian symbols, which seems rather miraculous in itself.

Much has taken me away from the book, the women, the well, over the course of the past year — but they have never gone far. I'm determined to see them through to the end. I've got to do it somehow or these voices could go on forever. I mean, The Bible is a big book. It contains — in every sense of the word — a lot of women. I could spend the rest of my life "doing" them. And my own voice could get lost along the way.

So here I am at Fairy Stone State Park with the books and the butterflies and the rain and a broken stove that keeps maintenance men trooping in and out of my precious isolation all day today. Trying to end what that whisper from Mary started it seems like forever ago.

....

Mary. Mary. Quite Contrary. How does your garden grow? Little did I know way back when, when I first put myself in Mary's metaphorical sandals, where she would lead me. And for how long. I didn't realize then how many of the women named in the New Testament were named Mary. I think now of the nuns at Our Lady Of Hungary, who were all Sister Mary Something-Or-Other. I think of all the women in my family, most of whom have Ann as part of their name. I think of how the Bible is full of *begats*, but usually overlooks the anonymous begetters. The moms. "Anonymous was a woman," said Virginia Woolf — an often quoted line that grows less true, I like to think, with every repetition.

I don't recall ever deciding to do this. But I let Mary speak. I started using my poetic license in a manner I never had before. I started listening to/making up voices, putting on masks, speaking in tongues that had been speaking to me, I suppose, since I was a girl. The rest, as they say, is *history*. But, as Mary first whispered in my metaphorical ear: *Don't believe a Word.*

Grace Notes

1. SPEAKING IN TONGUES — see *Genesis,* especially Chapters 1 and 11.

2. LILITH — see *Isaiah* Chapter 34, where the "screech owl" is supposedly the only direct reference to Lilith remaining in the Bible. According to Kabbalistic lore, she is the first wife of Adam who fled Paradise because she objected to always being on the bottom during sex. She is, according to some sources, associated with the Shekinah — the feminine presence of God. She is also seen as the dark side of the feminine, and held responsible for wet dreams, the deaths of infants in their cribs, but also their laughter in dreams.

3. EVE — see *Genesis* Chapter 2 with which I take liberties.

4. NOAH'S WIFE — see *Genesis* Chapter 6—10. Noah's wife was not given a name of her own, although I see her, no doubt, performing primary pet care on the Ark.

5. LOT'S DAUGHTERS — see *Genesis* Chapter 19. Lot, one of the few supposedly righteous men in town, offered his virgin daughters to the mob of Sodomites in order to protect the strange angels who came to lead him and his family to safety before the city was destroyed by fire. After their mother is turned into a pillar of salt (because she dared to look back) they lived secluded with their father in the mountains. They both managed to get him drunk and conceive children by him — apparently with him being none the wiser.

6. SARAH — see *Genesis* Chapter 16-22. She was the wife of Abraham, the first of the Patriarchs, who laughed at God when she heard him promise her husband she would

conceive a child in her very old age. She bore Isaac, who Abraham was willing to kill as sacrifice to prove his loyalty to God.

7. REBEKAH — see *Genesis* Chapter 25-28. She was the wife of Isaac, the second of the Old Testament Patriarchs, who despite his father's willingness to play with fire, grew to be a man. After being discovered at a well, she married him and bore twin sons, Esau and Jacob. She favored Jacob, who was younger by minutes, so she conspired with him to trick Esau out of his birthright and his father's blessing.

8. RACHEL AND LEAH — see *Genesis* Chapter 29-35. Rachel and Leah were sisters and both wives to Jacob, the third of the Patriarchs. Jacob loved Rachel, who was "barren," but was tricked into marrying her elder sister Leah first. Leah, though unloved, was remarkably fertile. Like her foremother Sarah, Rachel was "barren" until her old age — when she gave birth to Joseph (famous for his many-colored coat) and Benjamin, so she encouraged her husband to impregnate her maid, who she later had banished along with her children. Rachel died in childbirth.

9. MIRIAM — see *Exodus* Chapter 15 and *Numbers* Chapter 12. She was the sister of Moses and Aaron and said to be "a prophetess." When she and Aaron criticized Moses for marrying an Ethiopian woman, she was punished by being stricken with leprosy.

10. BATHSHEBA — see 2 *Samuel* Chapters 11-18 and 1 *Kings*. She was the wife of Uriah and later of David;the mother of Solomon. King David saw Bathsheba bathing on her rooftop and summoned her to him. He impregnated her and then conveniently arranged for her husband to be at the head of a battle, where he was killed. Their first child

died as punishment. Later, Absalom, a son of David's by another wife, plotted his father's overthrow. The Shunamite was a young virgin summoned "to keep David warm" in his old age. Though often portrayed as a "temptress," Bathsheba is also, in the Christian tradition, a direct ancestor of Jesus.

11. THE QUEEN OF SHEBA — see 1 *Kings* Chapter 10. The Queen of Sheba visited King Solomon, having heard of his wisdom. She came "to prove him with hard questions." After spending time learning from him, the Bible tells us "there was no more spirit in her." According to some legends, she later bore Solomon's son.

12. DELILAH — see *Judges* Chapter 14-16. She was the woman responsible for the downfall of Samson, who was noted for his strength. The source of his strength was his hair, which had never been cut. It was, in a sense, his Achilles' heel. Samson also had a weakness for riddles and bets, one of which led to the gruesome death by fire of his Philistine wife. After Samson lost his strength and his sight, he was tied between two pillars, which he collapsed upon himself and a crowd of his mockers when his untimely haircut started growing out.

13. RUTH — see *The Book Of Ruth*. Ruth was the daughter-in-law of Naomi, who, because of a famine in Bethlehem, had traveled with her husband and two sons to the land of the Moabites. The Moabites were considered idolators by Hebrews. Despite this, both Naomi's sons married Moabite women. After the death of her husband and both her sons, Naomi decided to return to her homeland. Ruth, who declared her loyalty to Naomi in the beautiful "Song Of Ruth" (*for whither thou goest, I will go....*) returned to Bethlehem with her mother-in-law, and married Naomi's kinsman, Boaz. She became the mother of Obed, who was the father of Jesse, who was the father

of David. Therefore, she too, is, in the Christian tradition, an ancestor of Jesus.

14. VASHTI AND ESTHER — see *The Book Of Esther.* Vashti was the first wife of the Persian King Ahasuerus. At a great banquet, where he and his guests drank for seven days, the king ordered Vashti, who was noted for her beauty, to dance for the crowd, which would have been a great breach of propriety for a woman of her position. Unlike Salome in the New Testament, she refused, and was banished as a result of her disobedience. She was to be an example to all the women of the kingdom who might consider saying no to a husband's demand. To replace his wife, the king gathered together all the "fair young virgins" of the kingdom, so he could pick a new wife. Esther, also known for her beauty, found favor with the king, and, not knowing she was a Jew, he married her. Esther, by following the orders of her uncle Mordecai, managed to manipulate the king into lightening the burden of her people under his rule, and at a crucial moment, revealed her true ancestry, saving the life of her uncle and the Jews who were being persecuted by the evil, Haman. She is celebrated at the Feast of Purim. Vashti disappeared from the story.

15. JUDITH — see *The Book Of Judith,* one of the Apocryphal Books. Judith was a widow, known for her beauty, as well as her wealth and her holiness. When the city of Bethulia was under siege by Holofernes, the general of the Assyrian King Nebuchadnezzar, she was one of the few who did not give up faith in God. She devised a plan to crush the Assyrians "by the hand of a woman." She adorned herself and left the city, passing herself off as a deserter. Like Delilah (and not unlike Esther) she used flattery to ingratiate herself to the man in power. One night, when Holofernes thought he would finally have his way with

her, Judith served the general wine until he passed out drunk. She and her maid then cut off his head and carried it back to the city in a feed bag. Thus "One Hebrew woman [has] brought disgrace upon the house of King Nebuchadnezzar."

16. SUSANNA — see *The Book of Susanna*, another of the Apocryphal books. Susanna was the beautiful young wife of Joakim. Two elder judges spied on Susanna as she bathed in the garden (echoes of Bathsheba). They accosted her and threatened to accuse her of adultery with another man, if she would not commit adultery with them. She refused, and they followed through with their threats, demanding that she be condemned to death for her transgression. The Judge Daniel cross-examined the two accusers independently, and since they did not get their stories straight (each claimed to have seen her under a different tree) she was exonerated and they were put to death as false accusers.

17. MARY/BETHLEHEM — See *Luke* Chapter 1-2 and *Matthew* Chapter 1. The traditional Christmas story.

18. ANNE — Though not specifically mentioned in the Bible, Saint Anne was, according to Catholic tradition, the mother of Mary, thus the grandmother of Jesus.

19. ELISABETH — See *Luke* Chapter 1. Elisabeth was the wife of Zacharias, the mother of John the Baptist, and the cousin of Mary. Like Sarah and Rachel in the Old Testament, she was well beyond childbearing years when an angel announced John's impending birth to Zacharias, who was struck dumb because he doubted God's word. John the Baptist later left home and preached the coming of the Messiah. He baptized Jesus himself, and was later beheaded.

20. SALOME — see *Matthew* Chapter 14 and *Mark* Chapter 6.

Salome was the daughter of Herodias and her first husband, and the niece of Herod, whom Herodias also married. It was this marriage that caused John the Baptist to condemn Herodias as a sinner. Knowing that Herod fancied her daughter, Herodias urged Salome to dance for him at his birthday, and when he publicly promised her anything in return, she asked (again at her mother's urging) for the head of John the Baptist. I imagine a possible past for both Salome and her mother.

21. THE PRODIGAL DAUGHTER. — See *Luke* Chapter 15 for the parable of the Prodigal Son, who left home as a young man and squandered his inheritance in debauchery. Finding himself destitute and living in a pig sty, he returned to his father to beg forgiveness and was welcomed with open arms. I imagine things turning out differently for a prodigal daughter.

22. THE WOMAN TAKEN IN ADULTERY — See *John* Chapter 8. A group of Scribes and Pharisees brought a woman caught in the act of adultery to Jesus and asked what should be done with her. According to the law, she should be stoned. In answer to their question, Jesus stooped and wrote on the ground (the only instance I know of where he wrote, though we are not told *what* he wrote) and then said, "He that is without sin among you, let him first cast a stone at her." No one did, and Jesus told the woman to go and sin no more.

23. MIRACULOUS WOMEN — 1) Jairus' Daughter — see *Matthew* Chapter 9, *Mark* Chapter 5, and *Luke* Chapter 8. Jairus approached Jesus and said his daughter was dead but he believed if Jesus would "lay his hand on her" she would live. Jesus said "The maid is not dead, but sleepeth" despite evidence to the contrary. He took her hand and the maid arose. 2) The Bride at Cana — see

John Chapter 2. The story of what is often considered Jesus' first miracle. He was attending a wedding where the hosts ran out of wine. At the request of his mother, Mary, Jesus turned water into wine. The bride is not specifically mentioned in John's account, but of course, there can't be a wedding without one. 3) The Woman cured of an issue of blood — see Jairus' Daughter. A miracle story within a miracle story. On his way to raise the twelve year old girl from the dead, Jesus encountered an older woman who had been bleeding for twelve years. Afraid to request a healing, she touched the hem of his garment, believing this would be enough to cure her. Jesus felt that "virtue had gone out of him," and the woman confessed her deed. Jesus said, "thy faith hath made thee whole." I see the three as fairy tale figures: maid, matron and crone.

24. PILATE'S WIFE — See *Matthew* Chapter 27. After the chief priests and elders delivered Jesus to Pontius Pilate, who had him scourged, Pilate's wife, who is not given a name, sent a note to her husband saying, "Have thou nothing to do with this just man, for I have suffered many things this day in a dream because of him." Ignoring her advice, Pilate "washed his hands" of the case, and condemned Jesus to be crucified.

25-26. MARY AND MARTHA — see *Luke* Chapter 10 and *John* Chapter 11. Mary and Martha of Bethany were sisters — to each other and to Lazarus, who Jesus raised from the dead. In this particular story, Jesus was at their house, preaching to a crowd. Martha, the practical housekeeper, was burdened with serving them all, while Mary sat at Jesus' feet and listened. Martha complained to Jesus that Mary should be helping her, but Jesus said, "Martha, thou art careful and troubled about many things: But one thing is needful: and Mary hath chosen that good part." This seems to be one of the stories that those who cite the Bible on "women's place being in the home" conveniently seem to forget.

27. MARY MAGDALENE — See *Matthew* Chapters 27-28, *Mark* Chapters 15-16, *Luke* Chapters 8 and 24, and *John* Chapters 19-20. One of the most colorful of the New Testament women. She is associated with the image of the "fallen woman" who finds redemption and with the woman who washed Jesus' feet with her tears and dried them with her hair — though according to John, that was Mary of Bethany. Luke says she was cured of demonic possession. She was one of the women at the foot of the cross, and the first to see Jesus after the resurrection. With the possible exception of the Virgin, this Mary is probably the most often mentioned woman in the the New Testament.

28. THE OTHER MARY — See *Matthew* Chapter 27: "And there was Mary Magdalene, and the other Mary, sitting over against the sepulchre." This other Mary is sometimes identified as the mother of James ("the less") and even as the sister of Mary, the Virgin, which would make her Jesus' aunt. She was one of the women who prepared Jesus' body for burial and was among the first to see him risen.

29. MARY — See *Matthew* Chapters 1 and 12, *Luke* Chapter 1, *John* Chapter 2 and 19. Mary was/is the mother of Jesus and, according to Catholic doctrine, is "the immaculate conception," who conceived Jesus and lived without ever "knowing" a man, including her husband Joseph.

30. VERONICA — Though not mentioned in the Gospels, Veronica, according to Catholic tradition, saw Jesus on his way to Calvary and took pity on him. She wiped his face with her veil and his image was miraculously imprinted on the cloth. The incident is commemorated in the ritual of The

Stations of the Cross.

31. THE WOMEN AT THE WELL — See various Bibilical stories
from both the Old and New Testaments. The folk song
refers specifically to the "Woman of Samaria," who in *John*
Chapter 4, conversed with Jesus and gave him water to
drink, despite the history of animosity between the
Samaritans and the Jews (also alluded to in the story of "the
good Samaritan"). Throughout the Bible, people — especially women — met their destiny at these watering holes.
Thus, the multiple voices in this voice.